GW01260607

Poems and Pictures - Christina Presents

Children's Poems
5th Anniversary Edition

An Invitation That Captured The Primary School Nation

Written by UK and UAE Children
Illustrated by Ric Lumb

Contents Page Number

WINNERS

Contents	Page Number

The Polar Bear
By Gigi Gebhard - Aged 9

The polar bear is feeling sad.

His home is melting, it's getting bad.

His icy world is far too hot,

We need to change or lose the lot.

Our beautiful planet is so fantastic,

Turn off lights, stop using plastic.

If we all play a little part,

The polar bear won't have a broken heart.

An Eight Line Rhyme WINNER

The Seasons
By Annabelle Butcher - Aged 7

In spring cute, cuddly animals are born.

I look at the flowers sitting nicely on the lawn.

Summer comes by,

It's really hot with no clouds in the sky.

Autumn is next, it starts to get cold.

The leaves fall off in colours of red, brown and gold.

The last season is winter and everything is bare.

Wrap up warm, it's freezing everywhere.

An Eight Line Rhyme WINNER

Painting a Rainbow
By Yanny Zaynchkovsky - Aged 9

The artist paints his picture in orange, yellow and grey,

A bright, scorching sunshine or a dark and drizzly day.

The artist paints his picture in brown, blue and green,

Silent, lonely landscapes or a lively city scene.

The artist paints his picture in red, pink and brown,

Funny, happy faces or an unhappy clown with a frown.

The artist paints his picture in black, bronze and gold,

If it's as perfect as a Picasso, he'll get millions when it's sold!

An Eight Line Rhyme WINNER

Music
By Fidha Labeeb - Aged 12

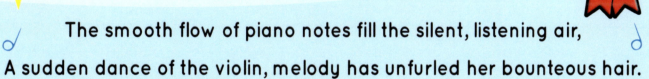

The smooth flow of piano notes fill the silent, listening air,

A sudden dance of the violin, melody has unfurled her bounteous hair.

Notes hit on, the listeners stare in a drunken trance of joy,

Every heart beats into the blooming music, either girl or boy.

Hark thou! Listen unto the stream of a marvellous duet played.

The joyful jumps and sharps and trebles, reminds me of dancing maids.

Slipping slowly high pitched notes blend into the flowing melody,

Enchanted minds, relaxing minds, heads nod in unison to the symphony

of midnight rhapsody.

Eight Line Rhyme Illustration WINNER

By Macaulay Paul Abrahams
Aged 10

An Eight Line Rhyme WINNER

Bouncing Bananas
By Millie Davis - Aged 9

Bouncing bananas, that's something I haven't seen.

Do you think they are related to the runner bean?

Bouncing is good for you, so are bananas.

They are certainly a lot better for you than pizza americanas.

If you eat some pizza, you must burn it off,

But don't just think you can eat and scoff.

Shall I bounce with it in my tummy, do I dare?

Anyway, my favourite fruit is still a pear!

An Eight Line Rhyme WINNER

The Earth Worm
By Rosie Kerven - Aged 8

1

He is a white noodle, slowly moving never to be found;

He is lurking in the shadows deep underground.

He slowly moves slithering on his belly.

The worm is squidgy, like strawberry jelly.

He is the farmer's friend, he helps things grow;

You never know there might be a worm working hard, deep below.

He moves up and down through the soil like a stitcher;

He is a superhero who munches the earth and makes it richer!

An Eight Line Rhyme WINNER

Creepy Crawlies
By Freya Murphy

1

Hello Mr Cockroach, where have you been?

Under the fridge where you can't be seen!

You scuttle around and across the floors at night;

When I come downstairs, you give me a fright

Big, bulging eyes and scary, flapping wings,

Long antennae - Yuk, I hate those things!

Please scutter away and leave me alone,

Why don't you find your own home!!!!!!!

Brian Banana
By Boyd Feather - Aged 8

Brian the Banana ran down the street.

He went round the corner and met his friend Pete.

Pete was delivering letters, he is a postman.

It was winter, and he was frozen!

Brian got some warm water to remove the ice.

'Thank you', said Pete. 'That was nice.'

And now that Pete was free,

They both went home for tea.

Route Healthy
By Isabelle Blackburn - Aged 11

Vegetables and fruit

Are the way to a healthy lifestyle route.

You have to eat healthy food;

If you don't, it will affect your mood.

Chicken, salmon, carrots and peas,

Beans, cherries and blueberries please!

These foods are important to have in your tum;

If you don't, you will get an enormous bum!

My Pet Pig
By Hugo Bainbridge - Aged 8

I have a pet pig who wanders about,

He has tiny little ears and a long squashy snout.

He has good hearing, just like a bat.

I must mention that he's incredibly fat!

Although he has no shovel, my pig loves to dig.

His favourite food to eat is a fig.

He eats the food I keep in a bag.

His favourite game to play is tag!

Kite Flight
By Matthew Way

One windy day, I was flying my kite.

A gust of wind blew with all of its might;

Up into the air I flew, what a fright!

Soon I discovered my worst fear was height.

I floated all the way to Louisiana,

Fell into a river and met a sharp-toothed piranha.

"Please don't eat me, here's a tasty banana.

I'd offer you lasagne, but it was stolen by an iguana!"

Croccy
By Millie Davis - Aged 7

His scaly skin is gross green.

He swims underwater like a submarine,

Out of sight, he cannot be seen.

He's a mean man-eating machine.

People run for their lives,

Because his teeth are shiny white knives!

He looks big, heavy, and slow,

But he's actually long, fast, and ready to go!

Healthy Lifestyle
By Bethany Draper - Aged 11

Running around makes you fit;

You don't even need a jogging kit.

Hopping, skipping and jumping too,

Whilst feeding animals in the zoo.

Exercising in the sun,

Simply just having fun.

Eating healthy every day

Will help you get fit your own way.

Flamingo Friday
By Mads Smith - Aged 10

Flamingo with chips,

Flamingo in dips,

Flamingo on toast,

And, of course, Flamingo roast.

Flamingo wings;

That goes with lots of things!

It's Friday! Hey jingo!

And I eat Flamingo.

Artists
By Amelia Milborrow - Aged 8

Lancashire was where Lowry was born.

Matchstick men are what were drawn.

Sunflowers is a painting by Vincent Van Gogh,

An artist who cut his left ear off.

In Spain lived an artist called Picasso.

He made a fifty foot sculpture for the people of Chicago.

Cézanne painted a picture of card-playing men

That was how they passed the time back then.

My Favourite Meal
By Nathan Twist - Aged 11

The dinner that I like most

Is my Nana Barnes' Sunday roast!

To start the meal with a bang:

Garlic prawns with a chilli tang!

Yorkshire pudding, beef, and peas,

Would I like seconds? Yes please!

Pudding is my favourite course,

Vanilla sponge with toffee sauce.

The Glacier
By Sophie Childs - Aged 11

Slowly but surely the ice starts to change,

Rocks reappear as the waters rearrange.

After millions of years the boulders touched by air once more,

But not a celebration as the light penetrates to the floor.

The glacier still slowly shifts, but this time with less mass,

Soon to no longer create a new valley with grass.

It is us to blame for this alteration of nature.

Without a change of heart there will no longer be a glacier.

The Jungle Tree
By Annie Cottle - Aged 7

Slinky tigers prowling round the thick, brown bark,

While cheeky, furry monkeys swing on the vines so dark.

Tweeting songbirds singing above the leaves

As rainbow-coloured butterflies flutter with the bees.

Tall, graceful giraffes search for lunch up high,

But small scuttery spiders search for theirs amongst the flies.

The home for all these animals is the sturdy jungle tree.

I hope they are happy, just like me!

Friends
By Lila Howard

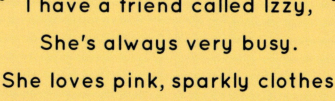

I have a friend called Izzy,

She's always very busy.

She loves pink, sparkly clothes

And ties her hair with big bows.

Willow is another friend at school,

She's clever, giggly and very cool.

Poppy is my loud and funny friend.

My teacher Mr Devitt wonders when the day will end.

Butterfly
By Charlotte Devney - Aged 8

Butterfly, butterfly, fly up high,
Fly up high in the sapphire sky!
Butterfly, butterfly, fly around,
Please don't make a sound.
Butterfly, butterfly, your wings are aglow,
Especially when you fly so low.
Butterfly, butterfly you're delicate and light,
Especially when flying towards the night.

My Mum
By Victoria Brumley - Aged 9

My mum likes to dance,
My mum likes to prance!
We skip together,
Whatever the weather!
Come rain or shine,
We move in time.
We dance to the beat
With flip flops on our feet!

My Furry Friends
By Amelia Baggott - Aged 9

My guinea pigs just love to munch;

Like eating machines, they gobble their lunch.

With knives for teeth, they chew and swallow.

They sprint so fast they are hard to follow.

Full of beans, they dash about,

Diving into tunnels and bouncing out.

As warm as a fleece, as light as a feather,

When the sun goes down they snuggle together.

Painting People
By Will - Aged 10

I paint in pastel colours and my favourite colour is blue.

I paint pictures of people, watching everything they do.

I paint people walking and talking,

And people laughing and singing.

Today is very bright with clear, blue sky,

With flocks of seagulls flying by.

The seaside is a busy place,

It puts a big smile on my face.

Scary Spiders
By Olivia Bielby - Aged 7

One day there was a spider under my bed.

It crawled on top of my head!

Mr Spider you're really big!

I think I'll call you Mr Jig!

So, Mr Jig, how are you doing?

Do you think if I stand on you,

you'll be ruined?   BOO!

When I get in bed at night,

You crawl over me and give me a fright!

Magical Music
By Sunetra Sen - Aged 8

Music is amazing,

It really is something.

Music can transport you to faraway lands,

It's almost as if you have magic in your hands.

When the music flows freely from your fingertips,

Wondrous words emerge from your lips.

When you learn to play music, it stays throughout

your life.

Music can get rid of your troubles and strife.

Ode to a Pancake
By Thomas Dart - Aged 11

Cooked to perfection, tossed in the air,

Caught in the pan and not in my hair.

This circle of chewy, tasty delight

Can be sprinkled with sugar, crispy and white.

Add sharp lemon juice, sweet raspberry jam,

Or savoury treats, like cheese and ham.

I can't wait to eat a pancake so yummy!

How many can I fit into my tummy?

Basketball
By Louis Bowen-Rayner

I once had a dream

About my favourite team.

We were able to fly

To play basketball in the sky.

To get the ball in the hoop

I had to loop the loop.

We won the cup.

Sadly I woke up!

Perfect Pizza
By Jake Chiappini - Aged 12

Pepperoni pizza is so divine,

It's the favourite food of mine.

Cheese, chive, and chorizo too,

It makes my taste buds go woo-hoo!

Pizza comes from a place called Naples,

And it's one of Italy's daily staples.

Perfect pizza is now a world phenomenon,

And I, for one, could eat it on and on.

Bikes
By Bethan Jellett - Aged 8

Two wheels on a bike,

Three wheels on a trike;

Round and round they never stop,

Children peddling until they plop!

I love riding on my bike

On a mountain hike.

In the sun, rain or snow,

Happily on my bike I go!

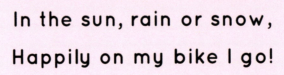

Pizza
By Tara Jayawardena - Aged 10

Crusty, flavoured, crunchy bread,

Smothered on top is tomato spread.

Cheese, ham, sweetcorn on top;

A pinch of herbs makes the pizza go pop!

The flavour explodes with a big bang,

When you taste the cheesy tang.

Wash it down with a fruity drink.

At the end of the meal the glasses go clink.

Clarinet
By Katie Rowling - Aged 10

I like to play the clarinet.

It makes me happy when I play perfect.

I can play so very fast

And make the notes last.

I can really play along to the beating rhyme.

I think I have a special touch to play on time.

I was born with a gift to play and play,

But everyone says it's the practice I put in each day.

Pizza
By Alex Hazelwood - Aged 12

It's pizza night and there ain't no stopping;

Loads of choices, as I'm adding my topping.

I finish with a flourish, sprinklin' on the cheese,

A few extra chillies; as much as you please!

Thin and crispy is the perfect pizza base.

Turn up the heat, the oven is the place.

Cooking time's up as we hear the pizza sizzlin'!

Get the napkins ready, the whole family's dribblin'!

A Window on Winter
By Ethan Howarth Wedgewood - Aged 10

Sat in front of a warming blaze

On the soft rug my cat Charlie lays.

Snow long melted from his fur,

Thoughts of snowflakes make him purr.

Long past sunset, dark outside,

Through bare trees a young owl glides.

How long will this crisp scene stay?

We'll never know until the next day.

Pigs
By Rhiannon Elwell - Aged 8

On our farm we have six pigs.

They are growing very big.

Where they live is full of mud.

Guess we are lucky there wasn't a flood!

The smallest one fell down a drain,

Getting her out was such a pain.

They climb in their trough when we give them their food.

No table manners at all, how rude!

Teamwork
By Evie Boettcher

Hi, I am Evie. I love to work as a team,

Especially with my friends, we always have a scream.

There's Alice who is funny,

And Annabel who's happy as a bunny.

There's Yasna who'd like to be in plays.

I've got so many I could go on for days.

We play and work so well together.

I hope we will stay friends forever.

Fish and Chips
By Abigail Neilson - Aged 11

My favourite dish has to be fish and chips,

Great with vinegar and a couple of dips.

Soft potato soldiers fried in a pan

Bring back memories of tea with Gran!

White fluffy flakes in crispy batter,

When it's brought out, it really stops the chatter.

To make this glorious feast a dream,

Add a dessert, and make it ice cream!

Exciting Bikes
By Ella Jellett - Aged 6

Exciting bikes all over the place,

I hope they remember to tie their lace.

Pedals going round and round,

I hope they don't hit the ground.

They go up the hill and round the bend;

If they fall, their race will come to an end.

My favourite thing is the view.

If you have a go, you will see it too.

Burger
By Alex Jeffries - Aged 11

Oh, the waft of sizzling beef,

Chargrilling from the flames beneath.

Lettuce, tomato, onion, and cheese,

Placed on the patty with the greatest of ease.

Ketchup, mustard, relish, and mayo,

Or add some chilli for a fiery volcano.

A towering stack of juicy flavour

For me to sit, chomp, and savour.

Do You Love Music?
By Logan Delaney - Aged 11

I love music, do you?

Playing an instrument is my favourite thing to do.

You can listen, write and play music.

If you have a special talent, you should use it.

A tambourine, piano, trumpet or guitar,

The sound of music can transport you afar.

It doesn't matter what music you like, rock, classical or pop.

It makes you want to dance and never stop.

23

The Sluggish Snail
By Jim King

The sluggish snail slowly produces slime;

He wriggles and wriggles for a very long time.

A bird comes close to the helpless creature,

Hoping to eat it with its beaky feature.

But the snail's shell is as strong as a rock,

So the bird, disappointed, has to dock.

The bird will definitely keep at bay,

So the miniature monster lives to slime another day.

What is the Solution for Pollution?
By Lily Rytwinski - Aged 11

Once trees lined grassy hills

And we saw pretty windmills.

Now litter covers the dirty streets,

No more happy, chirpy tweets.

Power stations polluting the air:

Are we cruel? Do we care?

Too much thick, smoggy pollution,

Surely there must be a solution?

Steak
By Josh Baggott - Aged 12

Steak is my favourite food.

It puts me in a brilliant mood.

When my dad turns the barbie on,

My hunger pangs will soon be gone.

I like mine rare, all nice and pink,

Not burnt and crispy, black as ink.

With mash or chips cooked nice and slow,

No veggies though to spoil the show!

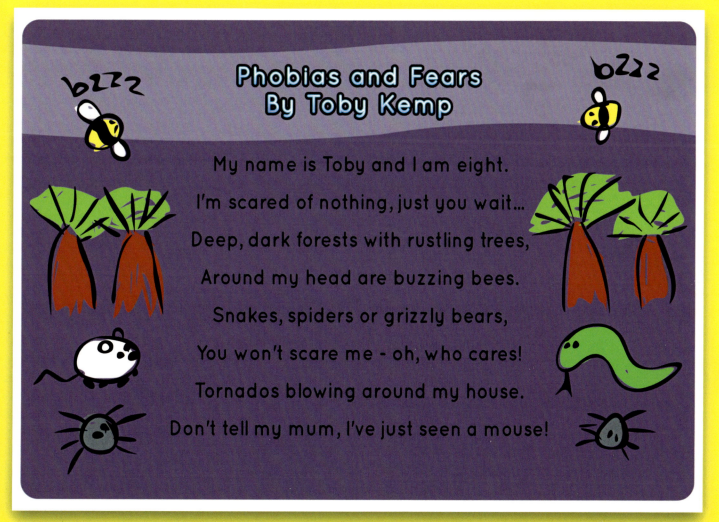

Phobias and Fears
By Toby Kemp

bzzz   bzzz

My name is Toby and I am eight.

I'm scared of nothing, just you wait...

Deep, dark forests with rustling trees,

Around my head are buzzing bees.

Snakes, spiders or grizzly bears,

You won't scare me - oh, who cares!

Tornados blowing around my house.

Don't tell my mum, I've just seen a mouse!

Butterfly
By Eleanor Rawcliffe - Aged 7

I am a butterfly,

I love to flutter by.

I go into the moonlight

On a dark night.

Colourful, pretty are my wings,

Through the air my fling.

Butterflies are attracted to flowers

And have really good collecting powers.

Exercise
By Charlotte King - Aged 10

Sometimes I like to exercise;

My dad says that I am very wise.

He says that it is good for your heart

And that it makes you smart.

I want to be healthy like my dad.

I don't want to be unhealthy and sad.

My dad says: "You can go fast or slow,

As long as you keep your get-up-and-go!"

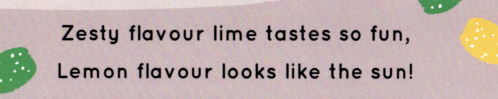

Fruit Pastilles
By Faith Budge - Aged 9

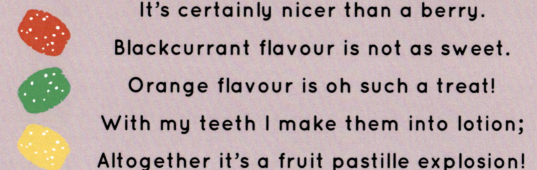

Zesty flavour lime tastes so fun,

Lemon flavour looks like the sun!

Luscious strawberry flavour is redder than a cherry.

It's certainly nicer than a berry.

Blackcurrant flavour is not as sweet.

Orange flavour is oh such a treat!

With my teeth I make them into lotion;

Altogether it's a fruit pastille explosion!

Gran Loves Glen Miller
By Annabelle - Aged 11

My gran used to dance to Glen Miller.

She said he was always a dance floor filler.

With the snazzy sound of instruments made of brass,

My gran said that this gave the music a 'touch of class'.

Through the music you can hear the saxophone,

Double base, drums and trombone.

My gran used to love jazz.

She said the music had pizazz.

My Favourite Quality Street
By Eleanor Bowen - Aged 9

Wrapped in a purple layered wrap,

Curled up at the ends like a bow on a hat.

A peanut buried in a heap of melted toffee,

With chocolate wrapped around, the colour of coffee.

The caramel so smooth and the peanut so crunchy;

The chocolate melts in my mouth and the flavour is lovely.

The purple one is my favourite sweet,

It is also my favourite Quality Street!

Season Special
By Clement Pravinata - Aged 7

Lots of people waving a palm,

Who also listen to a psalm.

Yellow is the colour of the summer flower

Powered by the strength of the solar power.

Leaves are falling from the tree to the ground,

Rotting away never to be found.

White is the colour of winter snow,

Falling from high to the ground below.

A Rainbow of Smarties
By Elizabeth Sykes - Aged 10

Red Smarties are like rubies and garnets too.

Orange Smarties taste like oranges (but there are only a few).

Yellow Smarties are like the sun on a sunny day.

Green Smarties are like meadows where we laugh and play.

Blue Smarties are like the sea where the sea creatures swim.

Indigo Smarties are like the sky when the lights are dim.

Violet Smarties are like flowers swaying with glee,

But any kind of smarties are the right ones for me!

A Worm in My Pocket
By Lilly Nopper

One rainy day on my way home from school,

I found a big worm and I thought it was cool.

I picked up the worm with my bare hand.

I held it up high, thinking how grand!

The worm was so cute and wriggled a lot.

I put him in my pocket to show my mum what I'd caught.

What will she say when I show her what I find?

Will she let me keep it? I hope she won't mind.

Dazzling Doughnuts
By Olivia Reid - Aged 9

Doughnuts have the most amazing taste,

Although you should not eat them with too much haste.

I love each individual sprinkle

And as soon as I swallow them,

my eyes begin to twinkle.

The smooth, sweet icing melted on top

Is known to make your heart suddenly stop!

And when you eat these doughnuts,

your heart sings out with glee;

Doughnuts are truly the best food for me!

Bing the Broccoli
By Levi Amy Johnson - Aged 8

Bing the Broccoli likes to run,

Bing the Broccoli loves having fun.

He likes to spend time ice skating

And is very good at weightlifting.

Mario Mayo is a friend,

Who drives Bing the Broccoli round the bend!

Bing likes to dance with Maria Mango;

When they get home, they do the tango!

Tacos
By Tori Hanson - Aged 10

All different foods put in a shell,

When you taste it, oh, it tastes so well.

Salad, tomatoes, cucumber, and meat:

This is a yummy tasty treat!

Tacos, you combine so many wonderful tastes,

Because of that, nothing ever goes to waste.

I like to eat them, hungry or not,

But beware, sometimes it can be a bit too hot!

Painting
By Isha Wider - Aged 10

Painting is lots of fun.

Go outside and paint in the sun.

I will show you how to draw in no time,

All you have to do is draw circles and a line.

I love art, everyone loves art!

My sister paints whilst eating a tart.

Art is elegant, so take it slow.

Oh I love it! Why not give it a go?

Chocolate Cake
By Heather Watson

I really do love scrumptious sweets,

But chocolate cake is better than any treats.

It does not take long to bake

A delicious chocolate fudge cake.

The rich chocolate sponge, so light and fluffy,

It rises in the oven making it lovely and puffy.

You have to try it, cake is the best,

Much more tasty than the rest.

Four Seasons in a Rhyme
By India Bryant-Chesters - Aged 11

Dancing daffodils sway in the sun

Easter is coming, it's so much fun.

On holiday with the family, hand in hand,

Making sandcastles on the golden sand.

Bonfire night fireworks shine so bright.

The Halloween pumpkins are filled with light.

Frosty mornings, nights dark and cold,

Curled up by the fire hearing stories of old.

Chocolate Cake
By Amber Dosanjh - Aged 11

Delicious tasty chocolate cake:

My all time favourite thing to bake!

Lathered in yummy buttercream,

It's delightful, a heavenly dream.

Covered in hundreds of coloured sprinkles,

Fills people's eyes with lots of twinkles.

Have a huge slice, don't eat with haste,

Its gorgeous, mouth-watering taste.

My Sister Molly
By Isabel Alice Cropper

My sister Molly is my best friend.

We like to play together and sometimes pretend

That we are famous rock stars playing to the crowd,

Making up our own songs and singing really loud.

Sometimes we fight and make each other cry,

Other times we are superheroes and I teach her how to fly.

I like to help my sister and I really love her lots

And even though she is naughty, she's the only one I've got.

Fajitas
By Ella Shaw - Aged 10

Fajitas are different from any other food.

If I don't have them, I get in a mood.

You can have it spicy, or even very mild;

I have chicken and tomato, and I make it go wild!

My mum likes it spicy and so do I.

My, my, have you tried it with steak pie?

A crimson red chilli finishes it off,

But then I get a tickle and a bit of a cough.

Things I Do
By Imogen Jane Hall - Aged 10

I swing my hips, I tap my feet,

I always dance to the beat.

When I am swimming, I feel alive,

Then I add a scuba dive!

Gymnastics is fun,

But I prefer to run.

I love to do ice skating,

Because it has a five-star rating.

Chicken Kiev
By Charlotte Inkster - Aged 10

A tangy kick, a taste to savour,

Oozing with garlic to add to the flavour.

A sprinkle of crumbs, a twist of herb,

It tastes so delicious, it is so superb.

A waterfall of garlic starts to appear,

When the core of the kiev is near.

Tender, juicy, you need it to eat.

It goes really well with chips and beet!

The Winter Festival
By Leah Green - Aged 11

I went to the Amy Johnson festival, it was fun.

I went with my bro, dad and stepmum.

It was very cold and the wind did blow,

But the Hull City of Culture put on a great show.

Images projected on Hull City Hall,

People of Hull were having a ball.

It's a cold winter's night, the fireworks explode in the sky,

All my family are eating and sharing a big meat pie.

Spaghetti
By Rudy Van Dort - Aged 10

Slithering like a serpent around my fork.

Something to look forward to after my walk.

Pink, juicy worms wriggling and jiggling on my plate,

Smothered in tomato sauce nobody can hate.

Oh how I love how it wraps around my fork,

Suffocating its prey till it can barely talk.

Oh how I love spaghetti!

It makes me go as wild as a yeti!

Teamwork and Friendship Fear
By Kara Burgess

Do you have friends who care?

Who will look out for you anywhere?

When your friends leave you out

Do you cry and clump about?

Do you stand there all alone

Wishing you were back at home?

Do you feel you are locked behind glass?

No one to talk to, no one to ask?

Spaghetti Bolognaise
By Charlotte Williamson - Aged 11

"Spaghetti Bolognaise":

What a wonderful phrase!

The way it wriggles like a worm

Makes you want to scream and squirm!

The yummy tomato sauce

Gives you... the force!

I like it with grated cheese;

It makes it the bee's knees!

Live Healthy
By Amirah Fathima - Aged 11

One, two, three, four, five:

Now I start my exercise!

Six, seven, eight, nine, ten:

I start to run around, and then...

Five, four, three, two, one:

I play a game of badminton!

Ten, nine, eight, seven, six:

I finish with some high kicks!

Ice Cream
By Lucy Brook - Aged 9

From the moment I come home, the air is filled with ice cream.

Sometimes I get so excited I jump around and I scream!

I taste the sauce, drop by drop,

But I quite often spill it on my brand new top!

I tuck in and taste the cherries carefully sprinkled around.

It makes my tummy rumble and the neighbours can hear the sound.

But when I finally reach the bottom, I slowly walk away,

I nag and nag my mum for more,

but she always shouts, "No more ice cream today!"

Reading Music
By Abigail - Aged 11

'Every Good Boy Does Fine',

Helps me to learn the notes on the line.

A treble clef, a quarter note,

Learning to read music gets my vote.

A bar line, notes and a rest,

A half note, a minim and other clefs.

The sound of music, a double flat, a sharp.

I'm learning to play music with the harp.

Sweets
By Louisa Moll - Aged 10

I love candy: it's a real treat!

There are lots of different types, lovely to eat.

Tasty, delicious, mouth-watering, nice:

If they weren't locked in a box,

They'd be gone in a trice.

Amazing, epic, best invention ever:

I will love them forever and ever!

Lollipops, boiled sweets, I don't really care,

As long as they don't get stuck in my hair!

Spring Time
By Harriet Gebhard - Aged 7

Can you hear the birds singing?

Can you see the lambs springing?

Can you see a bunny hop?

Can you find a white snowdrop?

Can you feel the rain showers?

Can you smell the lovely flowers?

Can you fly a kite in the breeze?

Can you see the blossom on the trees?

Victoria Sponge
By Isobel Maher - Aged 11

Victoria sponge is truly delicious.

When it disappears so quickly,

my mum gets suspicious.

It always makes my taste buds tingle,

All the wondrous flavours intermingle.

A sprinkling of sugar and a filling of jam,

Working out the recipe is like an exam.

I'm always ready for a slice of this cake,

It really is a brilliant bake!

My Best Friend
By Melissa May Power

I've got a best friend and I really like her.

When we're together, mum says 'you're hyper'.

If she sleeps over, we giggle, giggle, giggle.

In the morning all we get is tickle, tickle, tickle.

When she smiles, she looks so pretty,

Her clothes are smart and jewellery's glittery.

She keeps my secrets in a diary with a key.

Thank you, thank you, for giving her to me.

Chocolate Cake
By Sarah Ng - Aged 9

Rich and creamy, deliciously sweet,

The chocolate cake can't be beat.

It's so scrumptious, this chocolaty cake

And it's such wonderful fun to bake!

Whenever I'm feeling sad or down,

This dessert will get rid of that frown.

I love this amazing confection;

My name for it is almost perfection!

Football
By Lucy Blanchard - Aged 9

I love to play football in a team,

To play for England would be a dream.

To suddenly be praised,

Soon my coach would be amazed!

With my bright yellow boot

I came up with a shoot.

'Goal!' I shouted; it went in!

Afterwards I had a party with my kin.

Dino Diets
By Luca De-Giorgio - Aged 8

Herbivores eat plants,
But they don't eat ants!
Pterosaurs eat fish,
That's their only wish.
Carnivores crave meat;
Yes, that's what they eat.
Omnivores have it all;
Their food pile is very tall.

Season's Greetings
By Hannah Childs - Aged 7

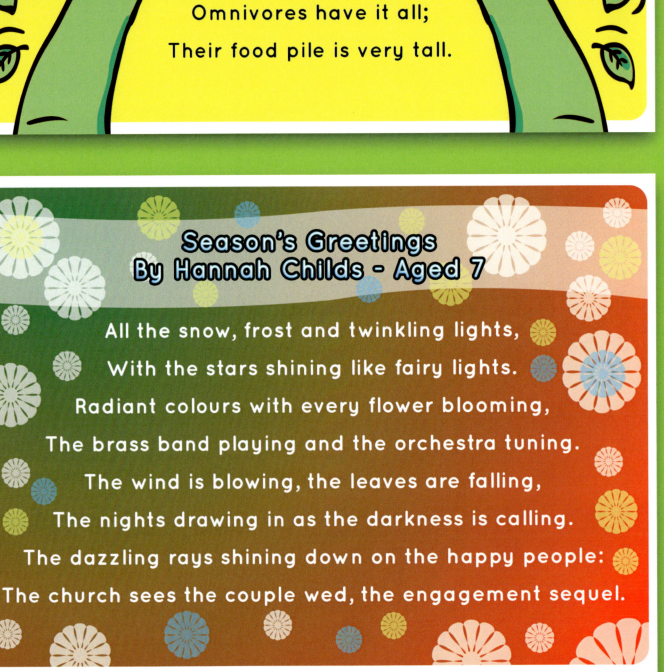

All the snow, frost and twinkling lights,

With the stars shining like fairy lights.

Radiant colours with every flower blooming,

The brass band playing and the orchestra tuning.

The wind is blowing, the leaves are falling,

The nights drawing in as the darkness is calling.

The dazzling rays shining down on the happy people:

The church sees the couple wed, the engagement sequel.

Food, Glorious Food
By Luca De-Giorgio - Aged 8

Pizza, burgers, junk food, yum,

All taste yummy in my tum.

Chocolate, sweets, chicken, fish:

Oh my gosh, what a delicious dish!

Strawberries, celery, sandwiches, cheese,

Oh mother, won't you please.

The more that I beg and plea,

Buy this lovely food for my tea!

Kings of the Rugby Pitch
By Nicholas Pleasance

I play for a team, the Kings under 8's.

Over the years we have become best of mates.

We train every week to be a great team.

Our mums and dads on the side lines do scream.

We run with the ball to score lots of tries.

We are always honest and no one ever lies.

But the best thing of all is winning a match,

Even if we get the odd bump and scratch.

Funny Bunny
By George Eastham - Aged 7

I am a bunny,

I look quite funny.

I think all day

In a very odd way.

My bobtail is big and furry;

Some might say it's scary.

I eat carrots and beans

That I pinch from Farmer Green's.

Handball
By Abdulla Albanna & Mohammed Almatroushi - Aged 11

Have you tried playing handball?

It's free to play, for us all.

The competition can be gruelling,

As nobody ever likes losing.

A great playmaker, defence and attack,

With some great left and right backs.

The circle runner creates openings

For teammates to take a shot at scoring.

Ladybird Love
By Casey Olive - Aged 7

Little ladybird please don't fly away,

Because I've loved you so much today.

Your little, red body with little, black spots

Looks like you've got the chicken pox.

As I lie here in the bath,

You crawl all over me making me laugh.

I am sad you flew away today.

It won't be the same without you, little May.

Mixed Seasons
By Khadija Khan - Aged 7

In autumn the leaves blow.

In the summer the grass does grow.

In winter with a frosty cold night,

The stars shine very bright.

The brown and orange leaves swirl

Gently as the winds makes them dance and curl.

In spring the flowers pop out,

Many colours all breakout.

Creatures
By Daisy Brook - Aged 7

On the wall there is a spider with terrible eyes.

I ask my mum to get rid of it. 'Ok' she sighs.

Not just the spider, there is a ladybird with a spot.

He flies around and about, when it is hot.

Bees hover around on the breeze;

The flowers they love make my sister sneeze.

Shimmering wings of the butterfly,

I stare at her beauty as she flutters by.

Friends
By Felix Fillingham

Friends are always around to play,

Even on a rainy day.

You can make up games and have some fun,

Do some painting or go for a run.

Climb some trees, go to the park,

Roast marshmallows when it gets dark.

Sometimes friends can stay the night,

And have a wonderful pillow fight.

Kenny
By Joe Lomax - Aged 7

My favourite animal is our pet sheep.

He came to live with us at just eight weeks.

He had to leave his mum because she couldn't cope.

We all loved him but our dad thought it was a joke!

My mum liked to carry him around and feed him from a bottle.

The lamb was called Kenny and followed her with a waddle.

Kenny loves to run and play, and is my best friend.

He now has a home for life and will be with us until the end.

Dribble, Shoot, Score!
By Saif Alshams - Aged 12

Dribble, shoot, score and celebrate!

As a team, we should all elaborate.

Football makes my body tense,

We need a plan that can make sense.

Skills and manoeuvres that seem impossible

Can make an amazing goal possible.

My favourite sport to watch and play,

Each and every single day!

Ice Cream
By Karli Twist - Aged 8

My most favourite thing to eat

Is a special seaside ice cream treat.

Layers of fruit, sauce and cream,

It's an ice cream lovers dream.

Scoops of ice cream, vanilla and berry,

Topped with whipped cream, sprinkles and cherry,

Crispy wafer, that's delicious.

It's knickerbocker gloryicious!

The Season of the Poem
By Aimee Dixon - Aged 7

The season of the poem.

The spring flowers are growing.

The summer sun is out to stay,

Let's all go out and play.

The autumn leaves are all around,

Red, yellow, orange cover the ground.

Winter brings the polar bear

And Jack Frost is everywhere.

My Favourite Creature
By Ellie Robinson - Aged 10

A lion stands proud on his ferocious paws,

Getting ready to catch his prey with his deadly claws.

He gets one step closer every day,

Tracking down his defenceless prey.

A flash of evil intent crosses his eyes.

The lion's opponent slowly and painfully dies.

Blood red as a ruby on his hands and feet,

As the lion cubs and he begin to eat.

Fears and Phobias
By Jack Chad

I spot a sticky spider's web,

Then I feel an itch on my leg.

Big, black and hairy too,

Eight legs, eight eyes looking up at you.

Crawling slowly across the floor,

Oh no, now its crawling up my bedroom door.

I start to panic in my head,

It surely won't crawl onto my bed ... Mum!

My Favourite Animal
By Chloe Mills - Aged 7

Turtles' shells are bumpy and lumpy,

Their flippers are long, their tails are stumpy.

The eggs hatch, the turtles must run,

Be quick, be quiet, get out of the sun.

The crabs and birds will try and get you

Or maybe the people from the zoo.

The lucky ones get to swim away

And play again another day.

Colin
By Rebecca Torkington - Aged 11

Colin the cricket bat

Was ever so fat.

He decided to exercise

And, to his surprise,

He became very lean

After joining the cricket team!

Colin became a star player;

He was so successful, they made him mayor!

My Favourite Dog
By Jack Fishpool - Aged 9

I have a border collie, his name is Tim.

I take him to puppy class to try and train him.

I always tell my friends it's fun to have a dog.

I get up early in the morning and take him for a jog.

We played a long game of tug of war,

I had to stop when my trousers tore;

I train him to be a goalie when we are playing football,

But he chews it to pieces and jumps rapidly over their wall!

Friendship
By Ella Baker

My friend is really funny.

She gave me her Stagg bunny.

She cheers me up when I'm upset,

She is someone that I will never forget.

We like to play on the swing.

We really like to laugh and sing.

I sometimes go to stay at night

And we have a pillow fight.

Animal
By Mabel Crozier - Aged 9

Guess what my favourite animal is?

Think hard, this will be a quiz.

It has big, black wings, it's a mammal too,

It goes hunting at night, for flies it can chew.

It has beady eyes and two pointy ears

That it uses to hear and to spot its fears.

It has sharp, little fangs glued to its jaw.

Can you guess what animal I adore?

I Love Food
By Abigail Draper - Aged 11

I love fruit, I love veg.

Carrot cake: I love a wedge!

Blueberry muffins, smoothies too:

I love these things and I've had a few!

Bouncing, jumping and skipping,

My friends and I are always laughing.

Exercise is lots of fun

For me, for you and everyone.

My Favourite Food, Olives
By Faye Atkins - Aged 9

Not many kids like olives, I think they're misunderstood.

I really wish they'd try them, I really wish they would.

Black ones are the best, they're shiny, red and plump.

I grab them from the olive jar and eat them in a lump.

No matter what colour, green, black or even red,

I'd eat them all day if I was allowed, until I went to bed.

Even then I think of olives dancing round in my dreams,

Red, black and green on different football teams.

I Fear Monsters
By Teva Hogarth

I fear monsters, they come out at night.

They creep away when the sun is bright.

The horrid creatures come from a bedtime story:

These putrid monsters are brainless and gory.

They have green teeth and black warts,

They make people have scary thoughts.

Some monsters make people scream.

I think they are very mean!

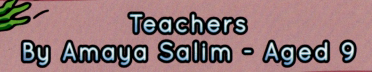

Teachers
By Amaya Salim - Aged 9

I think my teacher comes from Mars:

He likes to eat healthy fruit bars!

Singing, clapping, skipping, dancing,

All around the classroom, he loves prancing.

He shouts: "Get some exercise and eat healthy food!

It will put you in a great mood!"

'Okay Sir, we will', we reply.

'We will join in and definitely try!'

Healthy Food
By Aabid Anas - Aged 8

I like healthy food, it tastes so delicious.

My parents say it's very nutritious.

Apples, oranges, yum, yum, yum!

It feels so kind to my tum, tum, tum!

Healthy food makes us strong and grow,

It makes our skin all aglow.

So let's eat some healthy choices

And shout 'Healthy!' from the top of our voices.